GOOGLE DRIVE & DOCS 2016: Any Easy Beginner's Guide

Copyright © 2015.

What is Google Drive?

Google Drive is a free cloud storage solution for file storage and managements created by Google. It provides the capability and convenience of storing and accessing files anywhere using the cloud technology. Additionally, Google offers access to free web-based applications for creating documents, spreadsheets. You can also share files, edit documents, and spreadsheets remotely with several collaborators.

What is Google Docs?

This is a web-based program that allows you to create share and edit documents via a secure network system. Google Docs system allows users to upload word or tex based document to the system and change them to the online editing program. It has the capability of allowing several users in different locations to work on the same document in real time.

User can also store multiple versions of the document to be stored and accessed at any time without losing any information. The user can also determine the access level privileges given

Why use Google Drive?

Cloud storage has become quite common and currently Google Drive is one of the most recognized cloud storage services offered. It provides 15 gigabytes (15GB) of free storage space, you have the option of keeping your files online along with the flexibility of being able to access them from any computer with an Internet connection. Google Drive removes the need to email or save a file to a USB drive. The added advantage of sharing files also makes working with others much easier.

Google Drive Software

The Google Drive software that are available for the following devices are as follows: PCs running Windows

XP, Windows Vista, Windows 7, and Windows 8 with NTFS partitions, or Mac OS X 10.6 or higher; Android smartphones and tablets with Android 2.1 or higher; iPhones and iPads with iOS 5.0.

Google Drive and Docs is Appropriate for the Workplace

Google Drive is well suited for the workplace providir improved security and manageability of files. It provides the capability of archiving your company's email and web chat content for the period of time desired valuable for companies that require records t be kept for a certain period of time.

Offline Support

Google provides offline support there you can view, edit and create files without the need for internet connection.

Types of Files you can Create and Share

1. Documents: You can prepare your letters, flyers, essays, and other documents similar to Microsoft Word documents.

2. Spreadsheets: Great for storing and organizing information, similar in nature to Microsoft Excel workbooks

3. Presentations: Suitable for creating slideshows (example, Microsoft PowerPoint presentations)

4. Forms: Suitable for collecting and organizing data

5. Drawings: For creating simple vector graphics or diagrams

Creating a Google Doc / Google sheet

To use Google Drive, you must first create a Google account .These accounts are at no cost to the user. However, the following information will be required for you to create your account: your name, birthdate, and location. It should be noted that a Gmail email address is created simultaneously when a

Google account is created along with your profile.
If you had previously registered with Google, you do
not need to re-register, just sign in with your
Gmail information.

Create a File

A.   From your Google Drive, **Identify** and **choose**
the new button, then **choose** the file you want
to create.

B.   This new file will appear in a new tab on
your browser. Identify and select Untitled
document in the upper-left corner.

C.   The Rename dialog box will appear. **N**ame
your file, then click **OK**.

D.   Your file will then be **renamed**. Thereafter,
you may access your file at your convenience
from your Google Drive, where it will be **saved**
automatically.

E.   There is no Save button for your files as
Google Drive has auto save capabilities, it

automatically and instantly saves your files as you edit them.

Templates

This is a predesigned file that can be you can use to quickly create new documents. A variety of Templates are available on Google Drive Template Gallery, created by users. These usually include custom formatting and designs geared at saving time and effort when starting a new project. The objective of these templates is to help you create specific types of files, example, resumes or newsletters.

A. Several templates will appear. You can then browse templates by **category** or use the **search bar** to find something more specific.

B. When you have found a template you like, click **Use this template**. You can also click **Preview** to view it first.

C. A new file will be created with the selected
   template. You can then customize the file with your
   own information.

Google Official Template

To access templates submitted by Google:

A. **Navigate** to templates submitted by Google.

B. **Browse** and **select** the template of your choice.

Storing Files and Folders

You can easily store and access your file on the
cloud at your convenience via the internet. Google
Drive makes it so much easier and accessible to you.
You may also upload and edit your files from
compatible programs like Microsoft Word or Excel.

Free Storage

With Google Drive free storage space of 15
gigabytes, you can upload files to the cloud
repository. The categories of file that can be saved

on Google drive are as follows: files you can edit, (example Microsoft Office file) and files you cannot edit (example video).

Uploading files

You can upload files from your computer to Google Drive and if you are using the Google Chrome web browser, you are allowed to upload entire folders.

To upload a file:

A. From Google Drive, **identify** and **select** the new button, then **select** file upload.

B. **Identify** and **select** the file(s) you want to upload, **click** Open

C. The file(s) will be uploaded to your Google Drive.

D. You may be able to upload files by clicking and dragging a file from your computer into your Google Drive if your browser will allow.

To upload a folder:

You will only be able to access this feature if you are accessing Google Drive through Google Chrome.

A. **Click** the New button, then choose Folder upload.

B. **Identify** and **choose** the folder you want to upload, and then **click** OK.

C. The folder and the files within it will be uploaded to your Google Drive.

Converting files to Google Docs format

When you upload certain types of files (Microsoft Office files or PDF documents) you will only be able to view those files. If you want to **edit** these files in Google Drive, you will need to convert them to Google Docs format.

To Convert a file

Locate and **double-click** the file you desire to edit.

A. A preview of the file will be shown. **Choose** Open at the top of the screen.

B. The file will be converted to a Google document and will be shown in a new tab.

C. If you return to your Google Drive, you will notice that there are now two copies of the file—the original file and the new version in Google Docs format.

Managing your files

If you are finding it difficult to manage your file, there are a number of features that can be utilized to help manage and organize them. These features include searching and sorting files.

Searching for files

This feature allows you to search for specific files using words contained within the file or file name. In order to do this, locate the search bar, then type the word or file name you want to find. A listing of suggested searches and files will be reflected as you type. Click on a file to open it directly from the search results. You can also press the Enter key to see a full list of search results.

Sorting files

Your files are usually sorted from newest to oldest but you can use other types of sort to put your files in a different order. To do this select and click the Sort button near the upper-right corner of your Google Drive, then choose the sorting option required.

Applying filter

This feature allows you to hide files that are not currently required so that you can focus only on the ones you need.

To Apply a filter:

A. **Identify** and **choose** the search options arrow in the search bar.

B.   **Select** the filter you would like to use.

C.   **Choose** the desired filter

D.   **Click** the **s**earch button or press the enter key to apply the filter

E.   Only files that match the filter will appear.

F.   To remove a filter, **select** the text in search bar, then press the backspace or delete key.

Organizing your files

You may use folders to assist you in organizing and grouping your files, this feature work similar to the folders on your computer.

Creating a folder:

A. From Google Drive, **click** the n**ew** button, then select f**older** from the drop-down menu

B. An information box will appear. Enter a **name** for your folder, click **creates**.

C. Your folder will appear on the left below m**y drive**. You may need to click the d**rop down list** to see your folders.

To **move files into folders:**

A. **Click** and drag the file to your folder.

B. The file will then appear in the selected folder

C. To add more than one file to the same folder,
    press and hold the Ctrl key, then click to select
    each desired file. When you are ready, click and
    drag the files to the desired folder.

To Delete a file

This is similar to deleting a file from your compute
where you move the file to the Trash folder and then
delete it permanently.

A. Select the file you would like to delete, **click**
    the remove button to move the file to the Trash
    folder.

B. **Select** Trash in the left navigation pane.

C. The Trash folder will appear. **Click** Trash near
    the top of the screen, **select** empty Trash. The
    files will be permanently deleted

To Preview a file:

This function helps you to check if you are opening the right version of a file or to quickly view files without opening them.

    A. **Identify** the file you wish to preview, **choose** the Preview button.

    B. A preview of the file will appear.

Right-clicking

This is a shortcut that enables you to access the full list of actions for any file. Most of the actions listed here are available in other places on Google Drive.

Sharing and Collaborating files

You can share with your colleagues file(s) from your Google Drive. This will allow others to view and possible correct that same file. Although you can share with your colleagues any file saved on your Google Drive, it is important to note that the collaboration features can only be used for files created within your Drive.

Collaborator Sign In

In order to share a file with a small group of individuals, your collaborators will need to sign in to their Google account to view or edit the file however, for larger groups, or to make the file public, your collaborators do not need Google account in order to access the files.

To share a file with a limited group of people:

Identify and choose the file you would like to share, **Choose** the share button

An information box will appear, **Type** the email addresses of the persons you would like to share the file with in the people box. You may also add a message that will be emailed to the people you share the file with.

Thereafter, **Click** Send. Your file will be shared.

In order to have better control over your files, you can click the drop-down arrow to determine who can **edit, comment** on, or simply **view** the file.

Sharing with a link

It is very straightforward to share a file with a large group of persons. This can be accomplished by providing a link to the file of your choice in your Google Drive. A link can be very useful in instances where files are too large and therefore difficult to send as an email attachment, example music or video files. Additionally, you may share a file by posting the link on a webpage. As such individuals that click on this link will be redirected to the file.

To share a link:

A. **Identify** and **choose** the file you desire to share, **click** the share button.

B. An information box will appear. **Click** Get shareable link.

C. The link with the file will be copied to your clipboard. In order to share the file, you may then insert the link in an email message or on the Web. When you are finished, **click** done.

Files shared with you

There may be instances where persons want to provide you with access to a file. These files will be reflected in the incoming view. However, if you choose to access a file from Google Drive without switching to this view, you can move it. In order to do this, navigate to your shared with me folder, hover the mouse over the desired file, then select add to my drive.

Collaboration tools

If you share a file in a Google Drive format, you will have the option to allow your co-editors to change and edit the file. Google Drive provides many tools that enhance collaboration. This makes it easier to communicate with your co-editors and to see which changes have been made and by whom.

Revision History

Whenever Google Drive saves a document, presentation, or spreadsheet, a revision history is maintained, thi allows you to revert to earlier version of the document. In order to do this

A. Open the document, click **File** and select **See revision history.**

B. A revisions list is then shown on the right. Changes are color-coded for each collaborator.

C. Identify the version of the document you would li to revert to and click **Restore this revision.** Whenever you or your collaborators open it, the version that you have restored will be seen.

Headers and Footer

A. **Click I**nsert and select Header or Footer from the drop-down menu

B. **Type** your text within the header or footer dotted-lines area

Images

A. **Click** Insert and select Image from the drop-down menu.

B. **Select** from one of the following:

- Upload: Click Browse to select an image from your computer.

- Take a snapshot: Take an image of yourself.

- By URL: Paste an image URL you have found on the web.

- Your Albums: Select an image from your web album.

- Search: Search for an image on the web.

Adding Comments

A. **Highlight** the text that you wish to comment on.

B. **Click** Insert and select Comment from the drop-dow menu.

C. **Enter** you comment in the box that appears and **click** Comment.

Insert Links

A. **Click** the desired location that you want the link to appear.

B. **Click** Insert and select Link from the drop-down men Type the text that you want to be displayed as the link.

C. **Select** either Web address or Email address.

D. **Ente**r a URL or an e-mail address and click OK.

Add Drawings

A. **Click** Insert and select Drawing from the drop-down menu.

B. The Google drawing window appears. Create your drawing using the available lines and shapes from the toolbar.

C. To add the image to your document, click save and close.

Page Margins, Orientation, and Color

Adjust these settings by clicking **File** and selecting **age setup** from the drop down menu

Printing:

Click File and select Print. A PDF opens up ready for rinting. **Click I**nsert and select page number to insert age numbers.

Insert a Theme

A. **Click** Slide > Change theme.

B. **Click** on the theme of your choice to insert it int

your presentation.

Insert Your Own Background Image

A. **Click** Slide > Background.

B. **Click** on the Choose button.

C. **Click** Choose an image to upload to browse fo

an image.

D. **Click** Done to insert the image into your

presentation.

Insert Images

A. **Click** Insert and select Image from the drop-down

menu.

B. **Upload** an image from your computer or enter the UR

of an image you found on the web.

C. **Click** Select to insert the image.

Insert Tables

A.   Click on the slide where you want the table to appear.

B.   Click tables and select Insert Table from the drop-down menu.

Add and Delete Rows or Columns

A.   Right click on the column letter or the row number.

B.   A menu appears allowing you to insert and delete rows or columns.

Insert Formulas

Start by typing an equal sign **(=)** in any cell followed by the name of the function. Enter the first few characters of the formula you want to use and a list of the most relevant formulas appear below the cell. Click on the formula to insert it into your cell.

Insert Charts

A. Select the cells with data that you wish to include in your chart.

B. **Click** Insert and select Chart from the drop-down menu.

C. In the Start tab, you can edit the range of cells, select basic layout, and view recommended charts.

D. **Click** the Charts tab to select a new chart type.

E. **Click** Insert to add the chart to your spreadsheet.

Insert Gadget

A gadget is a mini program that interacts with the content of your spreadsheet.

A. **Click** Insert and select Gadget from the drop-down menu.

B. **Select** from a list of gadgets created by Google or by the public.

C. To add the gadget to your spreadsheet, click Add t spreadsheet.

Printing

Click file and select Print. A PDF opens up ready for printing. Click File and select Print settings to add pag number.

Conclusion

Google Drive is a very cost effective and convenient way to store and access documents, presentations, music, pictures, videos. It keeps your documents secured and reduces the incidents of losing important documents and files

In addition, Google Drive offers the capability to open files in formats that are not supported by your computer. These can be opened in a web browser and automatically search out and use the correct program to view the file.

CPSIA information can be obtained
at www.ICGtesting.com
Printed in the USA
LVOW04s0115130217
523966LV00041B/315/P